KT-394-201

06 Going wild

# SPRING
11

12 Spring signs
15 Growing food
16 Wild boat challenge
18 Underwater worlds
19 Nest building
20 Wild Easter games
23 Felting
24 Wild World Book Day
26 Celebrate forests
29 Magical mud
30 Camouflage games
32 Wildlife spying
33 May Day Queen
35 Dawn chorus breakfast adventure

# SUMMER
37

38 Wild sounds
41 Meadow minibeast hunting
42 Bush bugs
43 Natural stained glass
44 Nettles are nice!
47 Elderflower goodies
48 Fathers' Day challenges
53 Perfumes and potions
54 DIY summer festival
58 24-hour wildlife challenge
59 Make a wild bracelet
61 Wild swimming challenge
62 Butterflies
64 Wildlife after dark
67 Giant bubble games
68 Wild outdoor holiday games
71 Wild dolls

# AUTUMN
73

74 Wild walk jams
75 Blackberry tie-dyeing
76 Foraging bake-off challenge
79 Wild paints
80 Wild painting
82 Become a wild detective
84 Outdoor Halloween
85 Wild crowns
86 Wild music
87 Elf houses
89 Autumn jewellery
90 Leaf mobiles
91 Rainbow trees
92 Wild pictures
93 Boggarts
94 Leafy games

# WINTER
97

98 Story leaves
99 Wild snowballs
101 Icy decorations
102 Ice windows
104 Pictures in the snow
105 Broken ice sculptures and pictures
107 Snow sculpting
108 Snow and ice lanterns
110 Wild decorations
113 New Year's Day wild challenge
114 Wild winter games
116 Night games
119 Wild wintry beach adventures
120 Wild Valentine's Day

122 Wild safety
124 Index
127 Acknowledgements

# GOING WILD

This book is packed with our favourite Going wild activities, capturing the wonder and magic of every season. Have you ever played on the beach in the snow or got soaked to the skin in a summer rainstorm? Or tried star gazing while lying on the grass in the middle of the night? The wild world is always full of adventure and wonder; just be prepared for the weather and get outside!

We encourage families everywhere to get outdoors, seek adventure and take measured risks. You don't need to go on big expeditions to have fun; challenge yourself to try an outdoor mini-adventure every single week of the year, exploring the local neighbourhood as well as further afield.

## Wild adventure bag

Be prepared for spur-of-the-moment adventures by always having an adventure bag at the ready, packed with a few simple things. Don't overload yourself; you don't need much kit to have fun!

## Wild kit

Take a magnifying glass, bug box, plastic bowls and bags, old paintbrushes, an old sieve, some clay, string, a penknife, old gloves, a basic first aid kit and a water bottle. Don't forget to take a camera or smartphone and a little book for recording your adventures and discoveries.

### MAKE YOUR OWN WILD YEAR BOOK

Record your wild adventures all through the year. Make a feather paintbrush, paint with wild paints and stick in wild treasures and photographs.

## Summer kit

Don't get caught out – be prepared for everything! Pack the adventure bag with extra water, sun hats, raincoats, insect repellent, sun cream and tasty snacks.

## Winter kit

There's no such thing as bad weather, only the wrong clothes! Follow these tips so you can enjoy the wildest wintry adventures.

* **Footwear** Wear two pairs of well-fitting socks inside welly boots or sturdy shoes.
* **Warm clothes and waterproofs** Always wear several layers so you can shed a layer or two if need be. All-in-one waterproofs are perfect for wet days.
* **Gloves/mittens** Must be warm and waterproof; take an extra pair.
* **Hats** Always wear a hat, preferably with cosy earflaps.
* **Supplies** Take a few warming goodies – a flask of hot chocolate or soup, or baked potatoes wrapped in foil.

## Acorn ratings

We've graded each activity for difficulty and risk:

May be possible to do on your own

Some tricky bits which might need adult help or supervision

Involves the use of tools (such as a knife), or fire, or being near water, so adult supervision is essential

# SPRING

## What is special about spring?

The days are getting longer and temperatures are
rising, so shed those winter layers and feel the
first warm rays of sunshine.

Buds are bursting and green leaves are unfurling
as plants start to grow after their long winter rest.
The animal world is becoming more active; look out
for insects emerging and more birds flying and gathering
nesting materials. Try going into the woods at dusk;
the undergrowth is not yet dense and hibernation is
ending so this is the best time of year to look for mammals in the wild. Or just go outside in search
of spring surprises...

# PROJECT 01 SPRING SIGNS

How many spring signs can you discover? Here's a list of things to look out for, but you'll make your own discoveries too. Take photos to stick in your **Wild Year Book** (see page 7) or share with your **friends.**

Tick the boxes here, or take photos of other discoveries to share with your friends:

☐ Birds chirping and building nests

☐ Insects emerging to soak up the sunshine; look for butterflies, bees and ladybirds.

☐ Frogs and toads mating in ponds to produce their jelly-like spawn.

☐ Buds bursting and plants pushing their way up out of the soil.

☐ Tree flowers – catkins like little lambs' tails, furry pussy willow, tiny red star-like hazel flowers.

☐ Lizards basking in the sun.

**Challenge yourself** Can you spot ten different spring flowers?

**Picnic in the petals** Find a blossoming fruit tree; sit underneath it for a picnic and collect the falling petals for natural confetti.

# PROJECT 02 GROWING FOOD

**Home-grown food always tastes better. Try pots of herbs on a windowsill, carrots in a garden flower bed, or 'cut and grow again' lettuce in plastic boxes on a balcony.**

**A few tips:**

* Plan ahead; start growing in the early spring.
* Choose plants that are tasty but also quick and easy to grow; perhaps chives, spring onions or basil in pots, cherry tomatoes in a hanging basket or, if you have a bit more space, multi-coloured carrots, strawberries, lettuce or courgettes.
* Fill some pots with compost and sow your seeds.
* You don't need flower pots or a garden; compost in a few recycled containers works just as well. Be sure to pierce holes in the bottom of each container so they won't get waterlogged.
* To attract wildlife as well as grow food, choose nectar-rich herbs such as marjoram and thyme. These will tempt butterflies and bees later in the summer.

# PROJECT 03 WILD BOAT CHALLENGE

Challenge friends or family to make little boats from whatever you can find. Use natural materials such as leaves and twigs by a river, sea-washed rubbish at the beach or bits and pieces from the recycling bin at home.

Whose boat will float the best and travel the furthest? It's often the simplest boats that win. Look at these pictures for ideas.

## Boat building tips

❋   Use light materials such as corks.

❋   Make boats wider with outriggers.

❋   Add depth and reduce tipping by making a keel.

### SAFETY TIPS
- Be careful when playing by water.
- Always take boats made of non-natural materials home with you.

# UNDERWATER WORLDS

**Discover mysterious creatures in clean ponds and streams; no need for special equipment, just raid the kitchen cupboards!**

* Fill two plastic containers with water, placing them on level ground nearby.
* Move an old sieve slowly through the water, near to plants where animals may be sheltering. Empty the sieve into a container and look closely to see what you have caught.
* Use a paintbrush or spoon to transfer little creatures gently to cleaner water in the other container for a clearer view.
* Return the water, plants and creatures to where they were found, rinsing the sieve and containers carefully.

### SAFETY TIPS

- Always do this activity with an adult.
- Ensure skin cuts are covered with waterproof plasters.
- Wash hands thoroughly with soap afterward

# PROJECT 05 NEST BUILDING

**Some birds' nests look like untidy piles of sticks and others are finely woven and delicate, but each one provides a safe place to hold and protect eggs and baby birds.**

Could you be a bird? Test your nest-building skills.

＊ Collect building materials such as twigs, grasses, mud, moss, feathers, seed heads and sheep's wool.

＊ Weave bendy twigs in a circle to make a base. Line it with soft materials, perhaps wool and moss.

＊ To make a cosy cup nest, make a ball of grasses and pretend your fist is the bird's body, turning it round and round in the grass ball to make a bowl shape.

＊ Now make a bird from clay and feathers, just the right size to fit in your nest.

# WILD EASTER GAMES

**PROJECT 06**

**Get outdoors for some eggy games and activities.**

### Easter egg treasure hunt

✳ Prick each end of an egg with a large needle. Pierce the yolk to break it.

✳ Blow hard into one end, so the contents trickle into a bowl.

✳ Wash and dry the empty egg shells; decorate them if you wish and give each one a number.

✳ Write treasure hunt clues on small pieces of paper. Roll each one up as tightly as possible and push it inside a numbered egg.

✳ Hide the eggs in number order around the garden or at the park. Can your friends follow the eggy trail?

**Wild egg hunt** Can you find chocolate eggs hidden in wild nests (see page 19) around the garden or the park?

**Eggy games** Have fun and get messy: try egg rolling, egg boules and even playing catch with raw eggs. What eggy games can you invent?

**Egg decorating** Decorate hard-boiled eggs with paint, food colouring or tissue paper. Or draw on them with wax crayons or candles and soak them in food colouring for a patterned effect.

## WILD EASTER MOBILE

- Bend green twigs into circles, fixing them with florist's wire.
- Hang them together to make a mobile, resting a nest in one of them (see page 19).
- Decorate with blown eggs and chocolate eggs. Hang in a tree or over a table.

# PROJECT 07 FELTING

As the weather gets warmer, sheep shed some of their woolly fleeces. Look for wool strands on fences, thistles or other plants in sheep fields. Perhaps you can collect enough wild wool to make a felt mat to decorate with bought dyed wool.

* Comb wild wool into long strands (this is called carding).
* Place a layer of carded wild wool on a sushi mat or bamboo placemat, with the strands all lying in one direction. Add another layer in the other direction and then arrange coloured wool to make a picture or design on top.
* Cover the wool carefully with gauze or muslin. Pour very warm water and washing-up liquid on top, massaging it around to make foam.
* Peel back the gauze/muslin to check the wool is blending together.
* Roll everything up in the sushi mat, squeezing hard to get rid of as much water and soap as you can.
* Unroll and remove the felt. Rinse it once more and roll up in the sushi mat for a final squeeze before revealing your beautifully felted mat.

#  WILD WORLD BOOK DAY

**Celebrate the joy of books and reading with a wild World Book Day in early March.**

✳ Create an outdoor 'book nook', a secret reading hidey-hole where your imagination can roam free. It might be up a tree, in a meadow den, in a giant nest, or in a fort under the garden table...

✳ Make a fancy dress costume from some dressing-up clothes and a few wild materials. Perhaps you could become a witch, a warrior, a princess or the Gruffalo and act out your favourite book in the woods. Or make a wild mask, such as a Fantastic Mr Fox.

✳ Have a wild World Book Night and go out in the dark in your fancy dress outfits.

✳ Create special wild places to bring your favourite stories alive, like this outdoor room which looks ready for a Mad Hatter's Tea Party.

✳ Make a wild storyboard with pictures on the ground, like the one below, the tale *We're Going on a Bear Hunt*. Share storyboard photos with friends; can they guess your story?

# CELEBRATE FORESTS

 **International Day of Forests on 21 March celebrates the wonder of trees.**

Do you have a favourite tree? Why is it special to you? Do you climb it, sit among its roots, make dens under its branches, play in its fallen leaves or just enjoy its shade in the summer?

Trees give us clean air, wood and food, they support other plants and they provide food and shelter for minibeasts, birds and mammals. Celebrate them on this special day by planting a tree for the future. Choose a native species that will attract wildlife and won't grow too big for the space available.

**Tree planting tips**

* Push a spade into the soil, wiggling it backwards and forwards to make a wedge-shaped slit large enough for the roots.
* Place the tree gently in the hole, making sure all the roots are below ground.
* Holding the tree upright, push the soil firmly around the base of the stem with your foot. Give it a good drink of water.
* Name your tree and watch it grow. Water it in dry weather and don't let it be smothered by vigorous weeds.

# PROJECT 10 · MAGICAL MUD

Mud, otherwise known as soil, is a **vital** ingredient for all life on earth. Mud enables plants to grow, **and** they in turn provide food and shelter for animals, including **humans**. But mud isn't just useful: it's a lot of fun too. Get messy as **you discover** more about mud's magical qualities.

- ✳ Make layered mud cakes for wild celebrations.
- ✳ Dig up wild clay from unpolluted litter-free ditches. Mould it into creatures like hedgehogs and mice, or invent a wild monster.
- ✳ Have a mud bath and become a mud monster (it's good for the skin!).
- ✳ Go out in the rain; who can find the muddiest places to play Stuck in the Mud?

**PROJECT 11** CAMOUFLAGE GAMES

 Natural camouflage helps wild creatures hide from predators and prey.

## Camouflage yourself

✳ Wear wild-world colours with no bold outlines or logos.

✳ Use mud or face paint to change the colour and shape of your face.

✳ Find natural hiding places such as tree trunks, bushes and hollows.

✳ Can you stand tall to blend with a tree or curl up to mimic a tree stump or a rock?

✳ Keep to the shadows and move quietly and slowly without sudden jerks.

✳ Don't break the skyline; crouch down or crawl along the ground.

## Make a camouflage cloak

✳ Go to an area of woodland or scrub and collect bracken, grasses, leaves and twigs to weave or tie into garden netting. Cut a hole in the middle to make a poncho: your own portable hiding place!

## Camouflage game

✳ Invite your friends to the woods wearing wild-world colours.

✳ Make camouflage capes and paint mud on your faces and hands.

✳ Split into two teams. One team hides, using camouflage and behaviour to blend into the background. Can the other team spot their friends hiding in the woods?

#  PROJECT 12 WILDLIFE SPYING

**Go out at dawn or dusk and find a natural hiding place so you can spy on the wild world's shy creatures.**

• • • • • • • • • • • • • • • • • • • • • • • • • •

To make a wildlife hide, follow the BLISS formula:

**Blend** Find or make a hiding place to blend in with the surroundings.

**Low** Your hiding pace should not intrude on the view or break the skyline.

**Irregular** Follow nature's example; avoid straight lines.

**Small** The smaller the hide, the less chance of it being spotted.

**Secluded** Avoid busy paths; choose an out-of-the-way place.

### The no-hide hide

It's all up to you! Use camouflage (see page 30) and natural features to hide your shape.

# MAY DAY QUEEN

**The ancient May Day festival celebrates the arrival of summer by crowning a May Queen. This is the perfect time to make natural crowns (see page 85), garlands and necklaces of grasses, leaves and commonly found flowers ready to celebrate spring becoming summer.**

• • • • • • • • • • • • • • • • • • • • • • • • • • • • • • • • •

To make a flower chain, gather some flowers with their stalks – make sure the stalks are not too thin. Daisies and dandelions are good for this. With your thumbnail, carefully make a slit near the end of one stalk, and thread the next flower stalk through it. Carry on until you have a long enough chain to make into a flowery garland or necklace.

# DAWN CHORUS BREAKFAST ADVENTURE

**International Dawn Chorus Day on the** first Sunday in May celebrates nature's most spectacular music. **It's the** perfect time to get up early and greet the sun.

## Where to go

Go to the woods or a wooded park about an hour before sunrise, so you will be sure to hear all the performers as they arrive on stage. Find a good spot to sit, where you can make yourselves comfortable and enjoy the birdsong.

## Be prepared

* Take plenty of warm clothes and some cosy rugs to sit on.
* Record nature's concert on a smartphone; perhaps you could later set it as your early morning alarm or try to identify each bird's song.
* Take along an outdoor cooking stove or a fire pan, or make a small fire on bare ground, and cook up a hearty breakfast.

**SAFETY TIPS**
See the fire safety guidelines on page 122.

# SUMMER

### What is special about summer?

Summer is nature's rush hour, with all wild places working at full speed in the long daylight hours. Every meadow and wood, every pond, every garden and park buzzes and bustles with life.

There's something different to see every day: search for bugs and beetles, laze in the sunshine making record-breaking daisy chains or burying friends under freshly mown grass, or lie in a meadow and gaze through the stems to spot shapes in the clouds. On rainy days, shelter under leafy umbrellas, run barefoot through the sodden grass or search for stripy snails crawling among the wet leaves.

# WILD SOUNDS

**Discover nature's wild sounds early in the morning or just as evening falls.**

• • • • • • • • • • • • • • • • • • • • • • • • • • • • • • •

We only hear nature by escaping from the man-made sounds that normally surround us; mobile devices, traffic, TV, music and voices. Find a wild place to lie down, relax and listen. Perhaps you will hear buzzing insects, singing birds, a drumming woodpecker, a whispering breeze, a trickling stream, the squeaking of small mammals in the undergrowth, a chattering squirrel, or a falling leaf landing on the ground.

**Sleeping Lions listening game**
Invite everyone to lie down and close their eyes. Who can hear ten natural sounds? Who can be quiet for the longest time? Do you know which sounds were natural and which weren't?

# MEADOW MINIBEAST HUNTING

Crawl through long grass looking through a magnifying glass to discover miniature forests full of amazing creatures. Look closely and you may find caterpillars and grubs, ants, bugs and beetles, grasshoppers and crickets, even butterflies and moths.

. . . . . . . . . . . . . . . . . . . . . . . . . . . . . . . . . . . .

## Mini wildlife park

Mark out a small area with a string and twig fence – this is your mini wildlife park. Explore the park with a magnifying glass to find out who lives there.

## Sweep netting

Hold a large lightweight net at right angles to the ground and sweep it from side to side through long grass. Using a bug box or magnifying glass, take a closer look at the creatures you have caught and then return them to their habitat.

## How to make a sweep net

✳ Cut an old pillowcase in half, discarding the half with the opening.
✳ Sew or staple a hem at least 2.5cm/1in wide around the cut edge, leaving a small section of hem open.
✳ Untwist a wire coat hanger. Insert the wire into the hem opening, threading it all the way around inside the hem. Twist the ends together and tuck them inside.

# PROJECT 17 BUSH BUGS

Explore the bushes in the garden or the park to discover little creatures sheltering there.

※ Place an old tablecloth or sheet on the ground under a bush or tree, or ask some friends to hold it with you.

※ Shake the branches gently but firmly over the cloth and see who tumbles down. You might spot small flies and beetles, ladybirds, caterpillars and glossy green shield bugs.

※ Carefully collect the creatures in bug boxes so you can look at them more closely. Use a paintbrush to pick up the tiniest creatures.

※ When you've finished looking at the minibeasts, replace them carefully among the leaves where you found them.

# PROJECT 18  NATURAL STAINED GLASS

**Let the light shine through wild colours – nature's stained glass.**

* Find a green twig and bend it to make a circle. Tie in place with string or wire, allowing some extra length so you can hang it up.
* Fix some clear wide tape across the circle to make a 'window'.
* Collect fallen petals and other wild colours. Arrange them over the sticky tape and hang the coloured circle up outside a window.

You could also try this activity with coloured leaves in autumn.

43

## PROJECT 19 NETTLES ARE NICE!

Nettle stings may be a nuisance, but amazing nettle plants are good for wildlife and useful to humans.

### Nettles for wildlife

Wear gloves and sweep a net (see page 41) through nettles to discover caterpillars and other minibeasts.

### Nettles to eat

Wear gloves to pick tender young nettles to make a tasty soup.

✳ Fry an onion in butter. Add a chopped carrot, a chopped potato, half a carrier bag of washed nettles and 0.5l/1 pint of stock.

✳ Simmer for about 20 minutes. Blend and season.

### Nettle bracelets

Nettle fibres are strong yet flexible enough to make cord and even fabric.

✳ Wearing gloves, pick nettles in late spring or early summer and remove the leaves.

✳ Split the stems lengthwise. Open them out and bang them with a stone to soften.

✳ Peel back the woody pith from the middle, leaving the floppy outer fibres.

✳ Twist the fibres together to make a strong cord, or split them into three bunches and plait them. Wear as a wild friendship bracelet.

## DEAD NETTLES

Nettles can be useful all year round! The dead stems of nettles are lightweight and strong, perfect for kites. You may find them among nettle patches in the spring; if not, wait until winter when the nettles have died back. Make simple kites from plastic bags, nettle stems and thread.

## ENJOYING ELDERFLOWER CORDIAL

- Add still or sparkling water for a delicious drink.
- Mix a tablespoon of cordial with fresh strawberries or raspberries.
- **SORBET** Add 800ml/1.5 pints of water to 200ml/0.3 pint of cordial. Freeze for two to three hours, then mix well. Repeat this process three or four times to make a smooth sorbet.
- **FRUIT AND ELDERFLOWER SAUCE** Simmer plums or apricots in a little cordial and water until the fruit is cooked. Purée and pour over vanilla ice cream.

# PROJECT 20 ELDERFLOWER GOODIES

Creamy elderflowers burst open in **early** summer, perfect for making delicious cordial.

**A recipe for elderflower cordial**

* 1.8kg/4lb granulated sugar
* 1l/1.75 pints water
* 2 lemons
* 75g/2.5oz citric acid (available from good pharmacists)
* 25–30 large elderflower heads, washed

* Bring the sugar and water to the boil in a saucepan, stirring until the sugar dissolves. Turn off the heat.
* Grate the lemon zest into a bowl. Add the sliced lemons and citric acid.
* Cut most of the stalks off the elderflowers. Add the flowers to the bowl.
* Carefully pour the sugar syrup into the bowl. Cover and leave for 24 hours.
* Strain the mixture through muslin, squeezing out as much juice as possible.
* Pour into clean bottles. Store in the fridge or deep freeze.

**SAFETY TIPS**
- Always collect elderflowers away from roads.
- Be very careful when pouring hot syrup.

# PROJECT 21 FATHERS' DAY CHALLENGES

 **Fathers' Day falls around midsummer, the perfect time to share wild outdoor adventures. How about camping out, rain or shine – at a wild campsite, in the countryside with permission, or even in the garden? You could set Dad a challenge...**

## Sleep outside without a tent

❄ Try a hammock slung between two strong trees.

❄ Find a soft spot and snuggle down in a bivvy bag under the stars on a fine clear night.

❄ Make a sleeping shelter from natural materials, adopting someone else's den or building your own from logs and sticks with a covering of leaves.

❄ Make a DIY tent from a few strong sticks and a big plastic sheet or a tarpaulin.

## Light a fire without a match

❄ The best way to make a safe fire is in a fire pan or a fire pit.

❄ Make a tepee of kindling over a bundle of very dry tinder (wood shavings, birch bark, dried bracken, moss, grass or dry fluffy seeds).

❄ Now try to light the fire with a firestick (a steel rod attached to a flint). Hold the flint rod on the tinder and strike it at an angle with the steel; this should create a shower of sparks to light the tinder. May need a bit of practice!

*SAFETY TIPS*
See the fire safety guidelines on page 122.

**Bake bread over a fire**

✳  For a simple dough, mix 2 cups of self-raising flour with 1 cup
    of dried milk powder. Gradually add up to three-quarters of a
    cup of water, mixing steadily to make a non-sticky dough.

✳  Knead the dough on a board until elastic and smooth.

✳  Roll into sausage shapes and wind around sticks to cook over
    the fire, or make into a small loaf and bake in a clay flower pot.

✳  For ash cakes, mix self-raising flour with a little oil and some water.
    Mould into rounded shapes and bake directly in the fire. These
    are great for scooping up your curry!

**Cook supper over the fire**

Cook up a one-pot meal, such as a curry, in a Dutch oven (a cast-iron pot
suitable for putting in a fire).

# PROJECT 22 PERFUMES AND POTIONS

Go on a wild perfume hunt. How **many** different smells can you find?

## Summer potions

✻ Collect scented wild loose materials, perhaps petals, leaves and seeds.

✻ Mix them in a pestle and mortar with a little water and then pour into plastic cups.

✻ Name your potion and pass it around so everyone can have a good sniff.

## Secret smells

✻ Collect scented wild materials, **for** example flowers, fruits, pine needles, rotting leaves or wild herbs such as mint, thyme or marjoram.

✻ Put each material in a little bowl and crush it to release the scent.

✻ Everyone puts on a blindfold.

✻ Pass the bowls around; can **you** guess what is in each bowl?

### SAFETY TIPS
- These potions are only for smelling – strictly no tasting.
- Take care not to collect any parts of poisonous plants.

# PROJECT 23 · DiY SUMMER FESTIVAL

**A lovely warm weekend stretches ahead; get together with friends and hold your own mini-festival to celebrate summer.**

Find somewhere to camp out (see page 48), make a safe fire and share the wild world together. Here are a few fun ideas for some festival activities.

### Lantern making

✳ You will need lots of thin straight sticks, including some bendy green sticks.

✳ Fix sticks together with masking tape to make a shape; perhaps a cube, a pyramid, or an animal shape – maybe a fish or a bird. Fix a twig or string loop to the top of the lantern so that you can hang it from a stick.

✳ Attach a small torch or a glow stick to the base of the lantern.

✳ Stick colourful tissue paper over the lantern frame using diluted PVA glue or tape.

✳ Once the glue has dried, have a parade with the dramatic glowing lanterns.

### Fireside stories and treats

Some of the most magical outdoor moments are spent sitting around a fire with friends, sharing stories and songs under the stars, or gazing at the moon. Don't forget the marshmallows, so tasty when toasted on sticks over the fire.

**SAFETY TIPS**
See the fire safety guidelines on page 122.

## Glow stick games

Decorate yourself with glow stick necklaces and bracelets for a lantern parade, or draw pictures in the air and take photographs of the light trails.

## Face and body painting

Make natural chalk and berry paint (see page 79) and decorate each other's hands, arms and faces.

# 24-HOUR  WILDLIFE CHALLENGE

**Find** out about the wild plants and animals living in your garden, **on** your patio or in your school grounds.

✳ The aim is to record all the plants and animals you can find over 24 hours.

✳ Record your discoveries with drawings and notes or by adding examples of different leaves, petals and seeds.

✳ Many animals and birds are hard to spot but you may find clues – perhaps chewed leaves, feathers, fur, tracks or nests.

✳ Look for small plants and animals with bug boxes and magnifying glasses.

✳ After the challenge, photograph everything you have recorded. You could then compare with other places, or repeat the challenge in the same place at different times of year.

# MAKE A WILD BRACELET

Look closely at the wild world and **you** will find more colours than you can imagine. Go out on a **colour** hunt; can you spot all the colours of the rainbow?

- ✳ Cut a strip of card long enough **to** fit around your wrist, allowing a bit extra for fixing. Stick dou**ble**-sided tape over the card.
- ✳ Decorate the sticky side of the **bracelet** with little pieces of wild colour.

**Wild notes**

- ✳ Only collect tiny pieces of colour.
- ✳ Only collect colours from plan**ts if** there are plenty of them.
- ✳ Avoid poisonous or stinging **plant**s.

# WILD SWIMMING CHALLENGE

**How many different places can you try wild swimming in one year?**

You could swim in a clear, calm lake, explore a river pool below a waterfall, scramble through a mountain stream's shallow rushing water, wallow in a sun-warmed beach pool or swim after dark under a starry sky.

## Safe wild swimming

Only go wild swimming or wild paddling when you are with adults who know the water is clean and safe.

* Never jump into the water.
* Always swim near the shore and check tides and rip currents.
* Make sure there are safe places to get into and out of the water.
* Avoid fast-flowing deep water and never swim in rivers when water levels are high.

# PROJECT 27 BUTTERFLIES

**Hunt for butterflies; look for their symmetrical wing patterns and see how they sip nectar through their long straw-like tongues.**

## Make your own butterfly

✳ Cut some white card or a paper plate into a butterfly shape.

✳ Place strips of double-sided sticky tape over the body and wings.

✳ Make symmetrical wing patterns with wild materials.

✳ To make your butterfly into a feeder, fold aluminium foil into a long tray and stick this between the wings to form the butterfly's body. Fill it with butterfly food (see opposite).

## Make flower feeders

✳ Cut the top third off a clear plastic bottle and remove the cap. Cut the sides of the lower two thirds of the bottle into strips as shown.

✳ Bend the plastic strips outwards into a flower shape; paint them or stick on brightly painted cardboard petals.

✳ Place the bottle 'flower' into the inverted bottle neck. Push a straight stick into the ground or a plant pot in a sunny spot, and place the butterfly feeder over it. Put a small sponge in the bottle bowl for butterflies to stand on while feeding.

✳ On a sunny day, pour sugar syrup, mashed fruit or banana mush into the feeder and see who comes to visit.

## BUTTERFLIES' BANANA SMOOTHIE

- Mash a banana with a fork and add to a pan with 100g/4oz dark brown sugar and 200ml/7fl oz water.
- Gently bring to the boil and simmer until the mixture goes sticky.
- When the mixture cools, put it in a butterfly feeder. You could even eat any leftovers yourself!

# PROJECT 28 WILDLIFE AFTER DARK

Take a night walk and discover the dark wild world, when nocturnal mammals, moths, bats, glow-worms and owls emerge.

❋ **Plan your route carefully** Mark it with natural chalk arrows or glow sticks (if using glow sticks, take them all home with you).

❋ **Time your walk** Set off at dusk, the best time to see and hear night-time animals as they emerge.

❋ **Dress the part** Wear dark-coloured non-rustling clothing and quiet shoes. Camouflage your faces with charcoal or mud.

❋ **Remember snacks** Take some tasty food and a warm drink.

## Making the most of your night adventure

❋ **Night sight** Let your eyes adjust to the dark. If you must use a torch, cover it with red cellophane so it doesn't interfere with night sight and won't disturb wild creatures.

❋ **Listening game** Sit on your own and listen for night noises.

❋ **Stargazing** On a clear night, lie down in a dark open space and look up at the stars and the moon. They will look even better through binoculars.

❋ **Moth mysteries** Shine torches at a white sheet to attract these beautiful creatures on a warm, still night. If you are near an electricity supply, make a moth trap by cutting a 5l plastic container in half. Put broken cardboard egg boxes in the bottom and invert the top over it to act as a funnel. Shine a lamp over the trap; moths will be attracted to the light and then fall down the funnel. Release the moths gently once you have taken a closer look.

# PROJECT 29 · GIANT BUBBLE GAMES

**How to make the biggest bubbles you have ever seen!**

※ Thread cotton string through **two** 20cm/8in drinking straws, tying the two ends together and sliding the knot into the middle of one of the straws so you have a circle.

※ The straws must not be longer than the bubble mixture tray.

**Making bubbles**

※ Mix 4 parts washing-up liquid **or** baby shampoo with 4 parts rainwater and 1 part glycerine. Let the mixture stand for two hours or even overnight.

※ Pour the solution into a large shallow tray.

※ Dip the wand into the solution until the string is completely soaked. Hold one straw and slowly pull the rest of the wand out of the solution. Gently pull the wand through the air to form a long snakelike bubble.

※ To cut your bubble off, tilt the straw to close the gap between the strings.

※ Keep practising until you get the knack.

**Bubble tips**

※ **Weather** The best bubble days are still and humid; after rain is perfect.

※ **Type of soap/detergent** Try various brands of washing-up liquid and shampoo to find one that works really well.

※ **Foam is the enemy of bubbles** Always scoop it away immediately.

# WILD OUTDOOR HOLIDAY GAMES

**No** need to spend lots of money on activities; just get outdoors and make up your own games! Here are a few ideas to get you started.

### Knee volleyball

Mark out a playing area with sticks or rope, and a line on the ground to represent a net. Play like normal volleyball, but everyone must be on their knees. Great fun but hard on the knees and the jeans!

### Bums up

Everyone stands in a circle. One person throws the ball to someone else in the circle.

❋ If he or she misses the ball they go down on one knee. If they lose another life they go on both knees, then catch the ball with one hand. If they miss the ball again they must face a wall or fence with their backside up.

❋ Everyone else takes turns to throw the ball at the backside; whoever misses also has to make their backside a target. The game usually ends up with a line of bums against the wall and one delighted victor!

### Water fight

To make water bombs, half-fill a few plastic bags or balloons with water and use as ammunition. Make sure you pick them all up when the game is over. Large plastic bottles with holes in the lids make great DIY super-soakers.

# WILD DOLLS

As summer slips into autumn, the **fields** have been harvested and the grasses have set seed; time to make wild dolls from cereal stems and bunches of long grass or rushes.

* * * * * * * * * * * * * * * * * * * — * * * * * * * * * * * * * * * * * *

* ❋   Tie stems or grasses together in a neat bundle with raffia or string. Trim the ends with scissors or shears.
* ❋   Divide the lower half of the bundle into two sections to make legs and feet, then tie with raffia.
* ❋   Use raffia to attach a thinner bundle of straw or grasses at right angles to make arms.
* ❋   Weave in finer grasses, leaves or seeds to make details and faces.
* ❋   Alternatively, plait leaves or grasses together to make arms, legs and bodies for dolls.

# AUTUMN

## What is special about autumn?

Autumn creeps up on us as summer's heat slowly fades away. After the first hint of frost the leaves start to change colour as they prepare to fall. This is the time to play in crisp, coloured leaves, to raid conker trees, and to go out on misty mornings to discover glistening spider webs.

Autumn is also nature's harvest, with more wild food available than at any other time of year. Animals and birds feast and gather fruits and seeds, helping to spread plants to new places. Creatures of every kind begin preparing for winter; some migrate to warmer countries, while others fatten up to help them survive the cold months ahead. It's a great time to get outside and discover autumn's bounty.

# PROJECT 32 WILD WALK JAM

**Gather wild fruits such as blackberries, elderberries, bilberries, blueberries, raspberries, rose hips, wild damsons, plums and crab apples.**

❊ Gather edible wild fruits and a large leaf when on a favourite walk.

❊ Weigh and wash the fruit and then place in a saucepan with a little water.

❊ With adult help, bring the fruit to the boil. Add the same weight of sugar carefully to the pan. Simmer for about one hour or until it sets (when a blob dropped onto a cold saucer forms a jelly).

❊ Pour into a warmed jar. Decorate a label with pictures of the fruits and name the jam after your walk. Cover the lid with the large leaf.

❊ Try making jams from different walks; which walk tastes the best?

**SAFETY TIPS**
- Take care to collect only safe edible fruits and seeds
- Choose fruit bushes and trees away from roads.
- Get adult help when cooking hot jam.
- Never pour hot jam into a cold jar.

# PROJECT 33  BLACKBERRY TiE-DYEiNG

**Have you ever noticed how red your fingers and lips become after gathering and eating blackberries?**

✳  Find an old cotton pillowcase, some white cotton fabric or perhaps an old white cotton t-shirt. Use rubber bands to bunch the fabric into patterns.

✳  Put a handful of blackberries into a pot with some water and a few spoonfuls of salt. Bring to the boil.

✳  Place the prepared tie-dye items carefully into the simmering blackberry mixture, making sure every bit of them goes under the surface.

✳  After a few minutes, remove the items from the pan using a spoon or tongs. Rinse in cold water, and then remove the elastic bands to reveal the tie-dye design. Hang them on a line to dry.

**SAFETY TIPS**
Take care with the hot blackberry mixture.

# PROJECT 34 FORAGING BAKE-OFF CHALLENGE

How many wild foods can you find along the hedgerows, in the woods and in fields? Look for nettles, blackberries, raspberries, elderberries, rose hips, hazelnuts, walnuts, mushrooms, crab apples and wild herbs. Make sure you are out with someone who knows which wild foods are safe to eat.

• • • • • • • • • • • • • • • • • • • • • • • • • • • • • • •

The challenge

Everyone has to cook a tasty dish from wild foods and a few basic ingredients (such as flour, salt, milk, butter, sugar and eggs).

※ Find an outdoor space to make a simple outdoor kitchen and seek permission to make a fire in a fire pan or pit, or set up a barbecue. You will also need basic equipment like a griddle, frying pan and Dutch oven (see page 51), measuring cups, knives, spoons and a mixing bowl.

※ Choose a simple recipe like the delicious layer pancake opposite, which was made on a griddle. There is different fruit in each layer, including elderberries with sloes, crab apples with rose hips, and blackberries with damsons, all cooked with a little water and sugar.

※ To make your bake-off truly wild, decorate with leaves and present it on a bark plate.

※ Other bake-off suggestions might include blackberry cake baked in a clay pot or wild herb bread cooked in a Dutch oven among the ashes.

※ Award prizes for taste, wild presentation and the most creative use of foraged foods.

**SAFETY TIPS**
See the fire safety guidelines on page 122.

77

# PROJECT 35 · WILD PAINTS

**Become like one of the earliest artists, discovering wild paints by crushing wild materials to release colours.**

• • • • • • • • • • • • • • • • • • • • • • • • • • • • • • • • • •

The oldest cave paintings in the world were created more than 35,000 years ago from natural colours found in rocks, soils and charcoal. Nature is the source of many colours; collect wild materials, crush them with a pestle and mortar, mix with water and strain through a tea strainer or sieve to make smooth paints.

## Wild paint ideas

✳  **White** Grind chalk into a powder. Mix with a little water to make a paint.

✳  **Black** Use burnt wood, ash or charcoal; grind up and mix with water.

✳  **Purple and red** Try berries such as elderberries, blackberries, raspberries and rose hips. Squeeze through a sieve to make a purée, adding water if you need to.

✳  **Brown and terracotta** Collect mud and clay from different places; the colour may range from deep brown to a rich red. Or try boiling walnut cases in water to make a very dark brown.

✳  **Green** Crush grass and leaves to release green-tinged sap. If the green isn't strong enough, try boiling leaves with a little water.

See page 80 for some wild painting ideas.

**SAFETY TIPS**
Make sure you avoid poisonous berries.

# PROJECT 36 WILD PAINTING

 **Made some wild paints (see page 79)? Now get creative with them!**

* **Paintbrushes** Experiment with feathers, moss, dried grass or even your hands. Or make a primitive paintbrush by chewing on one end of a non-toxic twig to separate the fibres.

* **Wild canvases** Paint on large leaves, pieces of bark or wood, sticks, pebbles, a tree trunk, old slates or even the patio.

* **Inspired by Aboriginal art** Australian Aborigines tell stories through their art, often painting animals and intricate patterns of dots and lines, usually in natural colours.

* **Wild Year Book** Some of the more subtle wild colours, like grass green or rose hip red, may not work so well in the wild. Take them home and paint a picture, or print a pattern on paper or in your Wild Year Book (see page 7), as a reminder of your colourful autumn adventure.

# BECOME A WILD DETECTIVE

Most birds and animals are shy and secretive, but sharp-eyed wild detectives can spot the clues they leave behind.

**Wild food leftovers** Look for nibbled nuts, fruits and seeds, chewed leaves, broken snail shells, stripped pine cones, nibbled toadstools, bones and feathers. Can you work out who has been eating what?

**Pellets** Some birds, such as owls, tear their prey apart or eat it whole. Bones, fur and feathers are compacted into pellets which the bird coughs up later. Look for dry pellets below perching sites; pull them apart with tweezers to find out what the bird ate for supper.

**Animal pathways** Many animals use regular routes, perhaps between a burrow or den and a feeding ground. Can you spot animal pathways through the undergrowth? Look out for animal hairs where a pathway goes under a wire fence.

**Animal homes** Look for holes, nests and other animal homes: can you spot a wasp gall, spider's web, mouse hole, rabbit burrow, squirrel's drey or badger's sett?

**Animal poo** Many animals and birds produce very distinctive droppings; can you work out who produced which poo?

**SAFETY TIPS**
Only touch animal pellets if you are wearing gloves.

# OUTDOOR HALLOWEEN

For a magical wild adventure, make natural Halloween decorations and head off after dark to the woods, the park or the garden for a scary feast.

＊ **Halloween lanterns** Carve pumpkins into decorated lanterns and place them in a trail for your friends to follow. Or make lanterns in jars decorated with scary-face leaves.

＊ **Pumpkin faces** No carving involved, just stick on wild materials to bring them alive.

＊ **Leafy decorations** Cut coloured leaves into bat shapes and scary faces to decorate a hat or hang from the trees.

＊ **Prepare a warming Halloween feast:** cheesy baked potatoes and pumpkin soup, sausages wrapped in chunks of bread, toffee apples or apple tarts, and sweet pumpkin pie.

＊ **How about setting up a Halloween mystery trail with a few scary surprises?** Perhaps a ghost in the trees, a spider web across the path... Remember – no torches allowed!

# WILD CROWNS

**Gather golden leaves and natural jewels, like seeds and berries, to create beautiful wild crowns and crazy headdresses.**

• • • • • • • • • • • • • • • • • • • • • • • • • • • • • • • • •

Cut a strip of card and make it into a ring that will fit around your head. Stick double-sided sticky tape all round the outside and arrange your finds on your crown.

For a completely wild crown, weave leaves and flowers through a willow ring.

# WILD MUSIC

Discover natural percussion by experimenting with sticks, pebbles, seeds, nuts and other loose materials.

⁂ **Pebble percussion** In Hawaii, dancers tap pebbles together like natural castanets.

⁂ **Clapsticks** In Australia the didgeridoo is often accompanied by clapping sticks. Tap a strong stick against other sticks, stones and trees; how many different sounds and rhythms can you make?

⁂ **Wild xylophones** Hang up sticks of different lengths to make a simple xylophone, or experiment with lengths of plastic pipe or planks of wood.

⁂ **Wild maracas** Traditional maracas are made from dried gourds filled with dried seeds, shaken to make a rattling sound. Put dry seeds and nuts in jars to make DIY maracas.

ELF HOUSES

**If we had to choose our all-time favourite wild activity, it would probably be making elf houses.**

• • • • • • • • • • • • • • • • • • • • • • • • • • • • • • • • • • •

You can make magical elf houses wherever you are in the wild world, just using the loose materials around you. But perhaps the best elf houses are discovered and made in wonderful autumn woodlands at the foot of ancient trees, among twisted mossy roots and golden leaves. Let your imagination run free – who knows what little creatures might live here, only coming out when we're not around?

**PROJECT 42** # AUTUMN JEWELLERY

**Be inspired by nature's treasures to make precious wild jewellery.**

• • • • • • • • • • • • • • • • • • • • • • • • • • • • • • • • • •

Pack your bag with some thread (linen thread, wool or fine leather cord), needles, wire, a bradawl and equipment to make wild paints (see page 79). Here are a few wild jewellery ideas.

* **Rose hips** String along wire to make a necklace or a pendant. These look wonderful but won't last for long.
* **Leafy necklaces** Thread coloured leaves along a string.
* **Bark pendant** Scots pine bark flakes off in interesting shapes with swirly brown and grey patterns. Make holes with a bradawl and thread onto linen thread. Make a clasp from two acorn cups, one fitted neatly into the other.
* **Cone flakes** Paint the flakes with chalk paint (see page 79). Once the paint has dried, scratch a pattern into it with a bradawl or needle. Varnishing the flakes with diluted PVA glue will preserve the pattern.
* **Bracelets** Twist or weave grasses, nettle fibres (see page 43) or bendy twigs to make bracelets. Wire interesting seeds together or arrange coloured leaves on sticky card (see page 59).

**SAFETY TIPS**

Get an adult to help with using a bradawl.

# LEAF MOBILES

**Celebrate autumn's amazing colours with a bright mobile.**

✳ Pack a bag with twine, scissors and a large needle. Look for colourful fallen leaves in the woods or the park; how many colours can you find? Collect leaves, cones, a few seeds and a stick.

✳ Cut the twine into lengths of about 75cm/30in. Attach a cone or an acorn to one end of each piece of twine to act as a weight.

✳ Tie or thread leaves and seeds along the twine.

✳ Tie the leaf strings along a stick and hang them up to catch the autumn sunshine.

# PROJECT 44 RAINBOW TREES

**After the first frost, summer's tired green leaves begin turning gold, yellow, orange, red, purple and copper.**

Decorate trees with their own rainbow colours; here are a couple of ideas to get you started. Take photos of your masterpieces to share with your friends.

**Rainbow snake** Find a smooth winding snake-like branch, and attach leaves with natural blackthorn needles to make a patterned snake.

**Leaf flames** Cut coloured leaves into different shapes and pin them to the bark to make flame-like patterns up the tree, echoing the bark's pattern and texture.

**SAFETY TIPS**
Use blackthorn needles with great care; they are very sharp.

**WILD PICTURES**

Choose a special place to create wonderful wild pictures, then photograph them before they disappear. Perhaps your picture will be a roaring fire of bright autumn leaves, or a feathery fairy in a pine cone frame. Here are a couple more ideas.

**Leaf star and flower**

✳ Find some straight sticks and make a star on the ground (tip – make two overlapping triangles).

✳ Collect lots of leaves in different colours, shapes and sizes.

✳ Now colour in the star, arranging the leaves as you wish.

✳ Alternatively, make a flower shape with sticks and then fill in with colour.

**Woodland creatures**

Use twigs, pine cones and brightly coloured leaves to make a woodland creature; oranges and browns are good colours for a fox.

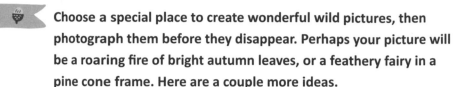

## PROJECT 46 · BOGGARTS

**Rumour has it that these mischievous spirits hide in the woods, playing tricks on anyone who comes to explore their patch.**

Perhaps the best protection is to make your very own scary, cute or funny boggart to scare the wild boggarts away.

* Wrap some well-worked soft clay around one end of a stick to make a head, moulding it to make features.
* Bring it to life with scary eyes and fierce teeth; is it wicked or cheeky?
* Decorate with leaves and other natural materials, including wild paint (see page 79).

# PROJECT 47 LEAFY GAMES

Catch a leaf as it floats down from a branch and you get to make a wish! Here are a few other leafy games to play in the woods.

## Special leaves

Among all those leaves, can you and your friends each find an individual special leaf?

❋ Choose one leaf; look at its shape and colour and feel its texture. Has it been nibbled? Does it have creatures living on it or inside it?

❋ Put your special leaves together; can you find your leaf again? If you describe it, can someone else find it?

## Blindfold leaf game

Each person feels a leaf while blindfolded. The leaves are put together and the blindfolds removed; can you find your leaf?

## Lurking in the leaves

Lie down on the leafy forest floor and look up at the trees. Place a few leaves gently over your face, and enjoy autumn's sweet musty scent.

## Leaf piles

❋ Rake and carry leaves with friends into enormous leaf piles; the bigger the better! It can be easier to carry the leaves in a rug or groundsheet.

❋ Take it in turns to rush into the leaf piles and hurl armfuls of leaves at each other.

❋ Lie down on the big soft mound and have a rug full of leaves emptied over you. Hide beneath the autumn blanket, before bursting out again.

# WINTER

### What is special about winter?

What does winter mean to **you**? Freezing mornings, cold grey days and long dark **nights**? Winter is all of these, but it's also the most thrilling time for wild adventures.

Try scrunching through **the** frost, tobogganing down snowy slopes, leaning into the force of a strong wind or running from **the** pounding waves on an empty beach. Scramble **up** into leafless trees to spy on the grown-ups, **peep** through ice windows or make snow creatures. **Don't** stay cooped up indoors; wrap up warm and **get** outside, ready to take whatever the **elements** hurl at you.

Winter is both an end **and** a beginning; look carefully and you will see signs **of** nature waiting patiently to burst into life at **the** first hint of spring.

**STORY LEAVES**

**Record moments and memories on leaves to hang in bare wintry trees.**

- - - - - - - - - - - - - - - - - - - - - - - - - - - -

✳ On a wintry walk in the woods, search for big leaves on the ground. Using a marker pen, write a wild memory, a nature poem or a very short story on each leaf.

✳ Find a bare tree in the garden or at the park to decorate with your story leaves, hanging them from cotton thread or fishing line.

✳ Perhaps other people will add their own memories and poems to the tree.

✳ After a couple of days, remove the leaves and thread.

# WILD SNOWBALLS

**PROJECT 49**

Snowballs with a difference; they **may** not last for long so take photographs.

* * * * * * * * * * * * * * * * * * * * * * * * * * * * * * * * * *

* **Decorate snowballs** Use loose natural materials such as moss, seeds, leaves and berries.
* **Hanging snowballs** Tie a length of string around a short stick and then make a snowball around the stick. Decorate as you wish and hang in the trees or outside a window.
* **Coloured snowballs** Fill spray bottles with water and a few drops of food colouring to make multi-coloured snowballs.

# PROJECT 50 ICY DECORATIONS

**Make the most of a cold spell by experimenting with icy decorations.**

If it's not quite cold enough for the decorations to freeze outdoors, put them in the freezer. Use a little warm water to help remove the frozen decorations from their moulds, before hanging them up outside.

✳ **Ice blocks** Fill containers with water and a few wild materials. Tie lengths of string around small pebbles and put one into each container, then freeze them.

✳ **Ice mobiles** One of our favourite activities, capturing wintry treasures in beautiful mobiles. Place biscuit cutters in saucers or jam-jar lids arranged on a tray. Put a little water and some wild treasures in each biscuit cutter, then lay a length of string to join them together. Freeze and then gently remove your mobile. Hang it up outdoors where it catches the light.

✳ **Balloon baubles** Pour water into uninflated balloons. Make wire holders by twisting one end of the wire into a thin spiral and then inserting into each balloon. Hang them on a washing line to freeze and then cut off the balloons to reveal beautiful baubles.

# ICE WINDOWS

**Here's a winter challenge: who can make the biggest ice window? What does the world look like through your window? Are there bubbles and patterns in the ice?**

* Pour water into a large bowl, or into a flan dish if you want a window with a crinkly edge.

* Fold a 50cm/18in length of string in half; hang the loop outside the bowl and place the loose ends inside.

* Arrange wild wintry materials in the water. To be sure they will be trapped in the ice, use materials that float or make sure the water in the bowl is very shallow.

* For a less natural but more colourful look, add food colouring.

* Place weighted plastic cups in the bowl if you wish to make holes in the windows.

* Leave outside overnight on a very cold night, or put in the freezer.

* When frozen, remove ice windows with the help of a little warm water.

# PROJECT 52 PICTURES IN THE SNOW

**Add to the fun of rolling giant snowballs by making giant pictures, words or snow mazes with the wiggly paths you leave behind.**

Choose a wide open area and start rolling a snowball. Rock it gently from side to side as you roll so it picks up as much snow as possible. If the snow is sticky enough a cleared track will be left behind you. Decide what you would like to 'draw' and then plan your route carefully.

# PROJECT 53 BROKEN ICE ART

**Everyone enjoys sliding and jumping on frozen puddles! And once the ice has been smashed, you can use the pieces to make ice castles, sculptures or pictures.**

If the weather isn't cold enough, make your own ice blocks in plastic tubs in the freezer.

Choose a natural canvas on the ground, a flat rock or a tree stump. Arrange ice pieces to make an ice person or an ice monster, perhaps with grass hair or a stick sword. Or make a three-dimensional sculpture – how about an ice dinosaur or a shining castle?

# PROJECT 54 SNOW SCULPTING

**What amazing sculptures can you make next time it snows?**

* Always use compacted snow; either roll giant snowballs, or pack snow into large plastic boxes and turn it out to make perfect building blocks.

* Carve and mould snow with gloved hands, a garden trowel or a beach spade. A knife or spoon is helpful for adding details.

* Keep standing back to view your progress, and make sure you build your sculpture on a sturdy base. It's tricky making animals or people with skinny legs, but you can always make a person or creature that is sitting or lying down.

* Add details to bring your sculptures alive; perhaps fearsome icicle teeth, pebble eyes or real antlers.

# PROJECT 55 SNOW AND ICE LANTERNS

Make magical glowing lanterns to brighten up dark winter nights.

## Snow lanterns

❄ **Giant lantern** Carve little holes all over a huge snowball. Place a nightlight in each hole.

❄ **Lantern trail** Arrange smaller snowballs in a line or a trail. Place a nightlight into a hole carved in the top of each snowball.

❄ **Lantern tower** Stack snowballs on top of each other to make a tower; push snow in between them to secure them in place. Put nightlights in holes cut in the side of each snowball.

❄ **Snowman lantern** Give your snowman spooky eyes!

## Ice lanterns

**Outdoor ice lanterns** Leave containers of water outside on a very cold night; by the morning you should have ice containers, perfect for beautiful ice lanterns.

**Freezer ice lanterns** Not cold enough outdoors? Try the freezer version!

❄ Put a heavy stone in a plastic cup inside a larger container half-filled with water. Slide leaves and seed heads down into the water.

❄ Place the container in the freezer for about 24 hours.

❄ Pour warm water over it until you can remove the ice lantern.

**SAFETY TIPS**
Always ask an adult to help you light candles.

# WILD DECORATIONS

Craft some wild decorations for a traditional Christmas tree or a favourite garden tree, or to string up outside a window.

## Twiggy stars

❄ Bend a supple twig in four places to make five equal lengths.

❄ Fold at each bend to create a five-pointed star. Tie the two loose ends together with fine wire.

❄ Decorate with silver or gold spray, ribbon or a length of ivy.

## Lanterns

❄ Wind fine wire around a jar, just below the rim. Attach another longer piece of wire across the top to make a handle.

❄ Decorate the jar with seeds, ivy, mistletoe, holly or other wild materials, using hot glue or tying things on with raffia.

❄ Place a nightlight in the jar.

## Honesty angels

❄ Bend a twig into a triangle, securing the ends with wire. Using a hot glue gun, stick honesty seeds over the triangle to make a dress. Add a poppy seed head for the angel's head.

❄ Make wings by gluing honesty seeds to a twig; attach the wings below the poppy seed head.

## Mystery animals

What wonderful creatures can you make from your seed collection?

## SEED AND BERRY RINGS, BAUBLES AND SPIRALS

Thread or glue seeds and berries onto fine wire. Keep the wire straight for baubles or bend into a ring. To make a spiral, wind wire around a broom handle and thread berries along the wire.

## SAFETY TIPS
- Take care when using a hot glue gun.
- Don't leave nightlights unattended.

# PROJECT 57
# NEW YEAR'S DAY WILD CHALLENGE

**Who is brave enough to bring in the New Year with a wild winter challenge?**

Challenge a friend or another family to one or all of the following.

* **Wild picnic** Have a picnic no matter what the weather, perhaps in an outdoor shelter.

* **Explore somewhere new** Go for an adventure somewhere you have never been before. You don't need to go far; explore your own area at random by tossing a coin every time you come to a junction. Where will you end up?

* **Barefoot challenge** Get in touch with the wild world through your feet: wade through cold muddy puddles.

* **Kettle challenge** Can you brew up some warming tea or hot chocolate on a hilltop or in the snow?

* **Watery challenge** Wade your way up a stream; who can go the furthest?

* **Discover natural climbing frames** Find a perfect climbing tree, a fallen tree or some rocks at the beach.

* **Wild wind** Make a wind flag so you can feel the wild wind.

* And finally – make a New Year's resolution to make space for a bit of wild time every day of the year!

# PROJECT 58 WILD WINTER GAMES

Some of our favourite wild games to keep you warm in winter.

· · · · · · · · · · · · · · · · · · · · · · · · · · · · · ·

### Flour grenade ambushes

✳ To make flour grenades, put a large spoonful of flour in some kitchen roll. Twist the paper around the flour and secure with masking tape.

✳ Go to the woods or the park with some friends and split into two teams.

✳ One team sets off ahead, perhaps laying a trail, and then lies in wait ready to ambush the other team. Or play as you wish!

### Wild tracking game

Make wild arrows from sand, grass stems, wood shavings, sticks, stones and fir cones. If there aren't enough loose wild materials, use flour instead. Agree a tracking code before you start; here are a few suggestions:

✳ **Straight or bent arrows** Go this way.

✳ **Cross** Dead end of a false trail.

✳ **Triangle** The trail could go along one of two paths.

✳ **Arrow placed over a stick** Go over an obstacle, perhaps a fallen tree or a stream.

✳ **Arrow with two arrowheads** The trail-laying party has split!

Split into teams; the trailblazers lay a trail, and then find a hiding place. The trackers wait for about 15 minutes before following the trail; can they find the trailblazers?

## CAPTURE THE FLAG WITH CATAPULT FLOUR GRENADES

- Make catapults by tying long modelling balloons between the forks of strong Y-shaped sticks.
- Split into two teams; each team chooses a base. Set up a flag between the bases.
- Each team tries to capture the flag, armed with flour grenades to throw or catapult at each other.

# PROJECT 59 NIGHT GAMES

**Don't let winter's darkness keep you cooped up indoors; try these fun night games.**

## Torch tag

✳  One person is blindfolded and equipped with a torch.

✳  Everyone else stands in a big circle around them and then tries to sneak up on them, moving as quietly as they can.

✳  The blindfolded person listens; if they hear a sound they shine the torch in that direction. If the torchlight falls on a stalker, he or she must stop still for 30 seconds before carrying on stalking.

✳  The game ends when the blindfolded person is captured by a stalker.

## Rope walks

Blindfold rope trails work well at night; if it's very dark there's no need for blindfolds.

✳  Set the trail up during daylight hours: wind a long rope through trees at about waist level, along a route with little or no undergrowth.

✳  Return after dark; hold onto the rope and follow the trail.

✳  Make sure there is an adult ready to meet you at the end of the trail.

## Glowing trail

✳  An adult lays a glow stick trail through the woods or at the park, making sure the trail is not too difficult to follow.

✳  Everyone else follows the trail, collecting the glow sticks on the way back.

✳  This could be played like wild tracking with two teams (see page 114).

## SAFETY TIPS
There should be an adult with each group,
or somewhere nearby.

# WILD WINTRY BEACH ADVENTURES

**Enjoy winter beaches with wild winds, pounding waves and a sense of freedom and space.**

✻ Feel the wild wind with a homemade windsock. Cut a bin bag and make it into a tube to stick around a large yoghurt pot with its base removed. Attach some string and decorate as a sea creature.

✻ Organise a wild skittles competition, throwing stones to knock down stone towers.

✻ Enjoy a winter picnic under a simple shelter tent or a tarpaulin.

✻ Make a small fire and cook up a fish dinner.

✻ Hunt for driftwood along the shoreline and whittle a beach memento.

**SAFETY TIPS**
See the fire and knife safety guidelines on pages 122–123.

# WILD VALENTINE'S DAY

Hunt for wild hearts or make a wild Valentine gift.

## Finding wild hearts

How many wild hearts can you find? Look closely and you may find them in leaves, pebbles, clouds, winter flowers, rocks, bark, lichens or mosses.

## Making wild hearts

* **Berry hearts** Thread berries onto wire and bend into a heart shape.
* **Moulded ice hearts** Find a heart shape and use it to make a plasticine mould. Put one end of a length of thin wire into the mould and add water; let it freeze to become an ice heart bauble.
* **Biscuit cutter ice hearts** Place heart-shaped biscuit cutters in a tray or saucer. Decorate with a leaf skeleton, a winter flower or some berries. Add a length of wire and some water; allow to freeze outside or in the freezer.
* **Snow hearts** Spray water coloured with pink or red food colouring around heart-shaped stencils on the snow.
* **Beach hearts** Make these from pebbles, shells, driftwood and other loose materials.

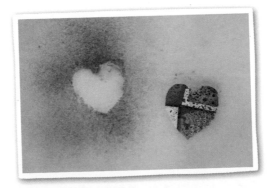

# WILD SAFETY

Have fun in the wild but please follow these guidelines, which will help you to stay safe and look after the wild world.

## Leave no trace
* Respect all wildlife and be considerate to other users of wild places.
* Whatever you bring out into the wild world, take it back home with you.
* Only collect plant materials that are loose or common and in abundance.
* Leave wild places as you find them.

## General safety guidelines
* Only use nightlights or candles under adult supervision and never leave lanterns unattended.
* Don't collect poisonous berries or plants.
* Wash your hands after working with wild clay, mud and other natural materials.

## Fire safety guidelines
Always follow this basic safety guidance when using fire.
* **Never** make fire unless you have permission to do so and adults are around to supervise.
* Make fires well away from overhanging trees and buildings.
* Make fires on mineral soil, in a pit or (preferably) in a fire pan.
* Never light a fire in windy or very dry weather conditions.
* Never leave a fire unattended.
* Have a supply of water nearby to put out the fire or soothe burns.
* Use as little wood as you can and let the fire burn down to ash. Once it is cold, remove all traces of your fire.

## Tool safety guidelines

✳ Only use a knife or sharp tools if you have been given permission and shown how to use them safely.

✳ If using a knife, bradawl, skewer, secateurs or any other tool always have a first-aid kit handy, and make sure someone knows how to use it.

✳ Make sure everyone is aware of the potential dangers of using sharp tools; accidents usually happen when people are messing around.

✳ Think about follow-through: where will the blade go if it slips? Before using a knife, make sure there is an imaginary 'no entry' zone all around you. To check, stand up with your arms spread out and turn around; you shouldn't be able to touch anyone or anything.

✳ Never cut over your lap – the femoral artery in the thigh carries large volumes of blood and if it is severed you will lose a pint of blood a minute.

✳ Work the blade away from your body, and away from the hand supporting the wood. Never cut towards your hand until you can use a knife with great control.

✳ Always cut on to a firm surface such as a steady log.

✳ If you need to pass a knife to someone else, always do so with the handle pointing towards the other person.

✳ Always put tools away when not in use; never leave them lying around.

✳ Knives should only be used when taking part in craft activities; a knife is a tool and never a weapon.

✳ Give knives and other sharp tools the respect they deserve: always stick to the rules.

# INDEX

## A
activity code 9
animals 18, 58, 64, 80, 82
autumn 43, 71, 73–95
   jewellery 89

## B
bark 48, 76, 80, 89, 91, 120
beach 6, 16, 61, 113, 119, 120
berries 79, 85, 99, 111, 120, 122
birds 12, 19, 58, 82
   nests 12, 19, 20, 21, 58, 82
   song 35, 38
blackberries 74, 75, 76, 79
boats 16
boggarts 93
bracelets 44, 57, 59, 65, 89
bubbles 67, 102
butterflies 12, 15, 41, 62–63

## C
camouflage 30, 32, 64
camping 48, 54
Capture the Flag 115
clay 6, 19, 29, 79, 93, 122

## D
dawn chorus 35
dolls 71
Dutch oven 51, 76

## E
Easter games 20
eggs 19, 20, 21, 76
   decorating 20
   eggy games 20
elderberries 74, 76, 79
elderflowers 46–47
elf houses 87

## F
Fathers' Day 48

feathers 9, 19, 58, 80, 82, 92
felting 23
festival 54
fire 35, 48, 51, 54, 76, 77, 119
   safety 122
flour grenades 114–115
flowers 12, 33, 53, 62, 85, 120
foraging 76
forests 26

## G
games 20, 30, 38, 57, 64, 67, 68, 94,
   114, 115, 116
glow sticks 54, 57, 64, 116
grass 6, 19, 30, 33, 41, 48, 71, 79, 80, 89,
   105, 114
growing food 15

## H
Halloween 84

## I
ice
   balloon baubles 101
   broken ice art 105
   decorations 101
   hearts 120
   lanterns 108
   mobiles 101
   windows 102

## J
jam 74
jewellery 89

## K
kites 45

## L
lanterns 54, 57, 84, 108, 110, 122
leaves 30, 33, 44, 48, 53, 58, 71, 74, 76, 79, 80,
   82, 93, 99, 108, 120
   colourful 43, 84, 85, 87, 89, 91, 92

leaf mobiles 90
leafy games 94
story leaves 98

## M

May Day 33
minibeasts 26, 41, 42, 44
moss 19, 48, 80, 87, 99, 120
moth trap 64
mud 19, 29, 30, 64, 79, 113, 122

## N

natural stained glass 43
nettles 44–45, 76, 89
New Year 113
night games 116
nightlights 108, 110, 111, 122
nuts 76, 79, 82, 86

## P

pebbles 80, 86, 100, 107, 120
perfumes 53
petals 12, 43, 53, 58, 62
pine cones 82, 92
potions 53

## R

rose hips 74, 76, 79, 80, 89

## S

seed heads 19, 108, 110
seeds 15, 48, 53, 58, 71, 82, 85, 86, 89, 90,
    99, 110, 111
shells 82, 120
Sleeping Lions 38
snow 6, 99, 113, 120
    lanterns 108
    pictures 104
    sculpting 107
snowballs 99, 104, 107
spring 11–35, 44, 45
    signs 12
stargazing 6, 64

Stuck in the Mud 29
summer 6, 9, 15, 26, 33, 37–71, 91
sweep net 41, 44

## T

tie-dyeing 75
tracking 114, 116
trees 12, 26, 30, 42, 48, 80, 84, 86, 87, 94, 98,
    110, 113, 116, 122
    planting 26
    rainbow 91

## U

underwater worlds 18

## V

Valentine's Day 120

## W

water 6, 9, 18, 26, 61, 113, 122
    fights 68
wild crowns 33, 85
wild decorations 110
wild detective 82
wild kit 6
wildlife 15, 26, 41, 44, 122
    after dark 64
    challenge 58
    hide 32
wild music 86
wild paints 9, 57, 79, 80, 89, 93
wild safety 122
wild sounds 38
wild swimming 61
Wild Year Book 9, 80
wind 113, 119, 122
winter 9, 45, 97–121
    beach adventures 119
    games 114
World Book Day 24

# ACKNOWLEDGEMENTS

A big thank-you to all the young people who took part in activities: Lily, Charlie and Toby R; Carolyn S; Clifford, Frankie and Anya C; Anna, Tim, Nicholas and Ella V; Fiona and Eliza N; Freddy L; Lucas R; Rebecca and Edward W; Anna, Laura and Ben W; Sophie T; Isabella G; Catherine F; Milly B; Tilly G; Rebecca M; Lydia, Helena and Lucian S; David C; Milly H; Christopher and Sienna W; Scott H; Danny, Jess and Natali K; Kate W; Rose P; Libby and George W; Lucy B; Hamish, Isobel and Oliver M; Alexander and Mimi D; Magnus G; Josh G; Milissa D; Scarlet R; Carla, Louie, Stan and Frankie C; Sam V; Ayrton and Edward K; Amy, Annabel and Matilda S; Megan S; Felix N; Laura V; Elsa, Freddie and Maggie G; Genki, Milly and Eva M.

Thanks to the University of Oxford Harcourt Arboretum, where some photographs were taken.

Many thanks to our husbands, Ben and Peter, and our children, Jake, Dan, Connie, Hannah and Edward, for their support and all the fun outdoor adventures we have shared over the years.

And finally, thanks to everyone at Frances Lincoln.

*The Wild Year Book*
© 2018 Quarto Publishing plc.
**Text** © Fiona Danks and Jo Schofield, 2017
**Photographs** © Fiona Danks and Jo Schofield
**Cover & interior illustrations** © Harriet Taylor Seed
**Design** Sarah Allberrey

First published in 2018 by Frances Lincoln, an imprint of The Quarto Group.
The Old Brewery, 6 Blundell Street, London N7 9BH, United Kingdom
www.QuartoKnows.com

A catalogue record for this book is available from the British Library.

ISBN 978-0-7112-3926-5
Printed and bound in China
9 8 7 6 5 4 3 2 1

Brimming with creative inspiration, how-to projects and useful information to enrich your everyday life, Quarto Knows is a favourite destination for those pursuing their interests and passions. Visit our site and dig deeper with our books into your area of interest: Quarto Creates, Quarto Cooks, Quarto Homes, Quarto Lives, Quarto Drives, Quarto Explores, Quarto Gifts, or Quarto Kids.